Born in London, A
at Mercers' Schoo.
an open scholarship to Oxford, he did two years National Service in the Royal Air Force, becoming a Pilot Officer, before going up to St Edmund Hall to read English Language and Literature.

Whilst still a business trainee, he wrote a sketch for a children's television programme starring Ronnie Corbett. This led to a career writing comedy sketches and scripts for TV comedy series, Saturday Night Spectaculars and Sunday Nights at the London Palladium for most of the top comedians of the day, including Ronnie Corbett, Bruce Forsyth, Dickie Henderson, Roy Castle, Arthur Haines, Jack Douglas and Joe Baker, Dick Emery, Irene Handl, Des O'Connor, and many others.

After several years of comedy scriptwriting, he drifted back into business. Working for a large American trading organisation, he travelled the world, until he and a few friends set up their own company trading in metals and minerals, and ultimately in oil.

Leaving business a few years later, he wrote *Shadow of the Titan*, his first novel, based loosely on his business experiences. Subsequently, he wrote *The Call of Destiny*, the first book in the Return of Arthur cycle, and its sequel, *The Hour of Camelot* and *Kill or be Killed*.

ALAN FENTON lives in London with his wife and quite a lot of Pekinese dogs.

ALAN FENTON

101 VERSES

Jim & Alix,

Have fun!

Best wishes,

Design and illustrations by Andrew Evans

www.alanfenton.co.uk

ISBN 978-1-5136-3641-2

Verses

Introduction

These verses are about a variety of things that either amuse me or trouble me about life – as, no doubt, they do many people.

Some are about things I love, like dogs, some about things I hate, like the hunting of wild animals, some are about belief and disbelief, some about faith, or lack of it, some about love of life and fear of death, some about my views (no doubt shared by many!) on politicians, and Scientific Advisers!

I had great fun writing them. I hope you will enjoy reading them.

ALAN FENTON

Good Days and Bad Days

There are good days and bad days –
More bad days the older you get.
But good days or bad days,
Every day tells me
It's getting late.
So even though it's a bad day,
It's still great!

Thank You, Lord

Thank You, Lord,
For the blackbird's song,
The lion's roar, The dog's bark.
Thank You
For sunset and sunrise, for music,
Love,
And laughter.

For the mysteries of the universe,
For all the things we know
And do not know
I thank You, Lord.
I don't believe in You,
But I thank You, even so.

My Life

Mine has been a bumble of a life,
With a trip here and a stumble there,
Never quite knowing who I was,
What I was going to be,
Or where I wanted to go.
And now that I'm near the end of it,
I still don't know.

People I wish I'd Known Better

Here are some of them . . .

Cleopatra.
Winston Churchill.
Einstein.
Chopin.
Shakespeare.
Dickens.
Toulouse Lautrec.
Mozart.
Jane Austen.
Dostoevsky.
Alexander the Great.
Sibelius.
Burt Bacharach.
Thomas Hardy.
Florence Nightingale.
Mary Queen of Scots.

My parents . . .

A Walk in the Park

Walking in the park
A stream of bird shit blanked my eye.
Was that an accident?
Or a message from on high?

Just a Dog

He was just a dog.
That's all he was, they said.
And of course he was just a dog.

But he was *my* dog.
And when I stroked him
I was stroking ten years of love,
Ten years of sleeping on my bed,
Ten years of walks in rain and shine,
Ten years of leaps and licks when I came home,
Ten years of life – his life and mine.

So yes, it's true.
He was just a dog.
But when my just a dog died
Part of me died too.

Other Worlds

Looking up
At all those other worlds
Hurtling a billion miles an hour through space,
You can't help wondering
If it's some kind of race.
What's their hurry?
Where are they trying to escape to?
Is there some place
They have to go?
Or are they just passing through?
That's what I'd like to know.
Wouldn't you?

If Only

I look back on my life and think
If only.
If only I'd done this.
If only I'd done that.
If only I'd been a better son,
Better father, better husband . . .
. . . Oh, a better everything.
If only.
If only my ears didn't stick out.
If only my hair had stayed in.
If only I were muscular.
If only I were thin.
If only.

If only I'd climbed Everest,
Won Wimbledon,
Or the Booker prize.
If only Jennifer Lawrence would beg me for a date,
Look deep into my eyes,
And tell me how great
My last movie was.
If only.

If only I were handsome.
If only I were tall.
If only I were better than I am.
If only this,
If only that,
If only the other.
And the biggest 'if only' of them all . . .

If only I didn't give a damn!

You up There!

You up there!
Yes, You. It's You I'm talking to.
Everyone says how great You are,
And what an outstanding job You've done.
Everyone but me, that is.
Well, there's always one, isn't there?

A couple of questions I'd like to ask.
First up . . . Could You please explain
Why You created us.
I don't want to be a pain,
Disrespectful or unkind.
But frankly I don't get it.
What on earth – or off it – did You have in mind?

Second up . . .I know I'm insignificant.
But is there any point at all to me?
And if there is, do tell.
What am I supposed to be?
What am I on earth to do?
I wish I knew.

All I know is – we are born, we live, we die.
And it's hello, world,
Goodbye.
Not much to be going on, is it?
Could I please be better informed
On my next visit?

Inhuman

You call cruel acts 'inhuman'.
But it's humans who commit them.
So why don't you call them 'human'?

You call barbaric acts 'bestial'.
But animals do what they have to do.

So what's so bestial about them?
And what's so human about you?

War

All those men – the bravest of the brave –
Who gave their lives
To save parents, children, wives,
If they could rise up from the grave,
I'd like to think they'd say,
'We know why we went to war.
We know what our sacrifice was for.
We did it then. We'd do it again today.'
I'd *like* to think it.
But you wonder, don't you.
You wonder.

The Fly

This fly
Dive bombs me in the kitchen.
Raising *The Times* to swat it,
'Die, fly! Die!'
I cry.
But hard as I try,
I never got it.

I saw it again the other day,
Crawling across the floor,
Buzzing its short life away.
I raised *The Times* to swat it,
But I couldn't do it.
I couldn't kill that fly.
So I closed the kitchen door
And left him to it.
Don't ask me why.

Who's Going to Wind the Clocks?

Who's going to wind the clocks
When I am gone?
Sort out the house at nights?
Tuck up the dogs?
Turn off the lights?
Who's going to do the things
I've always done?
Who's going to wind the clocks
When I am gone?

The Hunter

I shot a hunter in the fall,
And gave his neck a trim.
His head looks better on the wall
Than it ever did on him.

For many years I got my thrills
From shooting the big five.
I hunted them so successfully
Not one of them survive.

The wildlife I loved to kill
Is now impossible to find.
So instead of hunting wild things
I hunt the human kind.

The animals have disappeared,
But hunting is still fun.
So I'll go on killing people
Till my hunting days are done.

One Day More

I went to my local store
The other day
To buy some life.
But they don't sell it any more.
Or so they say.

I don't need a *whole* life, I told them.
Whatever scraps you have will do.
Give me a month –
Well, a month or two.

You're ***what!***
You're ***out of months!***
Right then, I'll have a week.
You surely can't be out of weeks.
You ***are!***
Make it a day, then, one lousy day!
A day is the least I'll take.
And I'm not leaving without it.

In fact I'll take a few
While I'm about it.
No days!
Not a single bloody day!

This cannot be true!
But it was.
It ***was*** true.
They promised to see
What they could do.
Come back in a week, they said.
Fat lot of good that was to me.
Next week I could be dead.

One Day You'll Come Looking

One day you'll come looking for me,
And I won't be there.
Not in town, or out of it.
Not upstairs,
Or down.
No doubt of it.
Not in my study,
Not in my chair.
Not anywhere.

Or nowhere you can find me,
However hard you try.
Where will I be?
I'll be where everyone goes
When they die.
Where's that?
God knows.

Monday

Friday's my apple pie in the sky day.
Monday's my doom and gloom
Day of the week,
Depressing and bleak,
The grouchy and grumps
Down in the dumps day.
I don't rate it.
In fact – I hate it.

I'd like to abolish it,
Polish it off,
Incinerate it,
Annihilate it.
I'd start the week with Tuesday
If I could.
Yes, Tuesday.
That'd be good.

The Man in the Mirror

There he is again –
The man in the mirror,
Stalking me,
Talking to me,
As if we'd met before,
As if he knew me.

Reminds me now and then
Of a man I used to know.
Though he was better looking,
More refined,
Eyes sparkling,
Face unlined.

There he is again,
Haunting me,
Taunting me,
Pushing me too far.
One day I'm going to ask him straight:
'Who the hell do you think you are?'

The Wall

I'm building a wall
Between me
And the incoming sea.

I'm building it tall.
But will it be tall enough?
For the wind blows strong,
The ocean's rough,
And I'm getting old.

How long will it hold,
My wall?
How long?

Mustn't Grumble

Tottering down the street
The old lady stumbled,
Tumbled and fell,
Grazed her knee, tore her skirt.
Helping her to her feet
I could see she was hurt.
But all she said was,
'Mustn't grumble.'

'Why not?' I cried. 'Why not?'
'You *should* grumble! You *really* should.
Grumbling's good!
Grumbling's good for you!'
'Yes, dear,' she said, smiling,
Stumbling bravely on her way,
Ready to tumble again
Some other day.

Brave Feebee

Little black dog,
Peering through tangled hair,
Mind that table, I say,
Mind that chair.

Blind you may be,
But you find your way
Without me
Telling your blind eyes
How to see.

No Sense

It makes no sense,
No sense at all.
Not one bit.
None of it.

Who has it easy,
Who has it hard,
Who rolls the dice,
Who picks the card.
Who is at peace,
Who is at war.
Who is rich,
Who is poor.
Who is blind,
Who can see.
Who laughs,
Who cries.
Who lives,
Who dies.

Why them?
Not me?

It makes no sense,
No sense at all.
Not one bit.
None of it.

My Dad

If I only I could talk to my old dad,
Give him a hug,
Tell him how sorry I am
For being such a bugger,
Sorry for the things I said
And didn't mean,
Make it all better,
Wipe the slate clean.

I'd like to have told him
What I had in my head,
What I wish that I'd said,
What I wanted to say.
But life is too short,
And death had it's way.

Heaven or Hell

I'd love to take my dogs with me
When I toss my lot.
Though I'll probably go to Hell,
And Hell is too damned hot.
So, please, whoever's in charge,
Bend the standing rule.
Give me a break,
And let me in upstairs
Where it's cool.
If not for my sake,
Then for theirs.

Sing a Song of Sixpence

Sing a song of sixpence,
A pocket full of rye.
Can anybody tell me
Why we have to die?
Like those poor blackbirds . . .
Was there poison in the pie?
And when the pie was opened,
Why? Oh why? Oh why
Did they thank Him for saving them –
The Baker in the sky?
Sing a song of sixpence,
A pocket full of rye,
Can anybody tell me
Why we have to die?

The Child is Father . . .

My father died an age ago
When I was twenty-nine.
If I could meet him now and then,
And chat of this and that,
Of where and when,
Would I be his father?
Or would he be mine?

Archaeology

Amazing the things you find
When you dig:
An ancient pot,
A coin or two,
A hoard of gold,
A Roman shoe,
Skeletons in crypts,
Frescoes and manuscripts,
Carving on walls,
Crossbows and cannon balls,
Gems for your cabinet,
Pots for your shelf.
Why – if you dig deep enough,
You might find yourself.

Home

I expect I'll be off now,
Or off very soon.
No idea where I'm going.
Think I'll start with the moon.
Then out into space
And a float through the stars,
With a side trip to Jupiter, Venus or Mars.
And then . . . ? What happens then . . . ?
Will I float there for ever
In the great astrodome?
I'm sure it's impressive,
But I'd rather be home.

The Next One

It takes a long time
To climb this high,
Day after day,
Year after year.
It takes a lifetime
To reach the sky.

And when you get there
The wind blows cold,
The sky's icy clear,
And the seagulls cry
That the end is near
In the by and by.

Up on the cliff top,
Perched on a life edge,
Watching the rocks
Fall into the sea,
You wait and you wonder –
Will the next one be me?

My Dog?

I own this mutt . . .
But . . .
I don't get to choose
If he's up for a walk,
Or down for a snooze.
If it's salmon or sole
In his finicky bowl,
Or a lamb bone to crunch
For his majesty's lunch.
Nor do I have the right
To decide every night
If he sleeps on my bed,
Or outside in the shed.
And I don't have a clue
What he's going to do
When I throw him a ball.
Will he come when I call?

So it's true,
Must be true
That I do
Own this mutt.
But . . .
Let me see . . .
Is it me who owns *him*?
Or him who owns *me*?

God Song

That's God out there
On the garden gate,
Fluffing out His wings,
Bowing to His mate.
And that's Him singing.
How beautifully He sings, does God.
You'd think He was a blackbird.

Do I?

Do I believe in God?
There are times when I do,
And times when I don't.
There are times when I will,
And times when I won't.
So do I believe?
Well, what can I say?
It depends how I'm feeling that day.

Night and Day

Because they all say it
Doesn't make it true.
Because they all do it
Doesn't make it right.
Whatever they say,
Whatever they do,
Day is still day.
Night is still night.

The End Game

They call it the end game,
The time to say goodbye game,
The time not to cry game.
There've been many more before you.
There'll be plenty more the same.
It's nothing new, my friend.
All beginnings have an end.
We're just passing through,
Fulfilling the universal plan.
So join the queue,
And take it like a man.

Hello God!

Hi there, God! If You're there?
Cheers!
Here's to You.
And here's to me
Drinking a glass of wine or two,
Or possibly three,
Thinking about life,
My hopes and fears,
When I hit the target,
When I missed.
Maybe you could help me, God.
If You exist.

Just joking, God. Of course You do.
We could have a chat,
Me and You.
I'd ask about this and that.
You could tell me what life's for,
What the future has in store,
Whether things get better or worse.
You might even explain the universe!

We could have a laugh,
Shed a tear or two.
I've plenty of those to spare.
Hello, God! Are You up there?
Are you awake,
God?
Give me a break,
God!
Until the day you do,
God!
I'll keep trying to get through.

Second Time Around

If I had another shot at it,
I'd bet you a penny to a pound
I'd do a damn sight better
The second time around.

But to be fair,
When I get my second innings
Just be sure you're there,
To hand me my winnings.

With Apologies to William S.

When that I was and a little tiny boy,
With hey, ho, the wind and the rain,
My brothers went to fight a war,
And never came back again.
Now that I've come to man's estate,
I tell my brothers every day –
'Don't go! Don't go!
Please won't you stay!'
But it's all too late, too late, too late.
And they wouldn't have listened anyway.

Remember?

Do I remember Christmas?
How could I ever forget?
Of course I do. And yet . . .
Actually, come to think of it, I'm not sure.
It's all so far away.
Or possibly so near.
Was it yesterday?
Or last year?
Or was that Easter?
Could have been.
Or was it Halloween?
And now, in the wink of an eye,
We're on the brink.

On the brink of what?
Spring?
Summer?
Autumn?
Winter?
And where's Christmas?
Remind me once again.
Gone! Not possible! When?
And was it *this* Christmas?

I can't remember?
Or the last?
It's hard to keep up, it goes by so fast,
Does Summer,
Autumn,
Winter,
Spring.
Does everything.

The Tree

See how it stands,
That tree,
So tall and proud,
Feet in earth,
Head in cloud,
Scarred by lightning,
Lashed by rain,
Bowed by wind,
Upright again.

Dying in gold,
Reborn in green,
Think what it's heard,
And what it's seen.
Dumb it may be,
But it speaks to you,
And it speaks to me.
And it's telling us both
A thing or two.

Chocolate Cake – a Cautionary Tale

And now for dessert . . .
For goodness' sake,
There's – yes, you guessed it –
Chocolate cake!
Chocolate cake and vanilla ice.
Yum yum, yummy! That sounds nice!

But then in my head
The arguments start.
Have a sorbet instead,
Cake's bad for your heart.
But I'm thin as a rake!
And I don't give a fig!
So why can't I eat cake?

Thin! You're not thin!
You're fat as a pig!
And being fat is a sin.
Everybody knows that.

So, do I?
Don't I?
Will I?
Won't I?

Make the ultimate mistake,
And eat the forbidden chocolate cake?
Yes, I will!
No, you won't!
Yes, I will!
No, you won't!
You're right! You're right!
My trousers are tight!
I'm putting on weight.
I'll ask for the bill
Before it's too late.
No, I won't!
I'm going to order the chocolate cake!

Big mistake! Huge mistake!
You must stick to your diet!
I will not! I want cake!
But they bake it in fat!
I don't care if they fry it!
I know what I'm at,
And I'm going to try it.
But then . . .
Oh, shit!
Shit!
Shit!
Shit!
They just sold the last bit!

That very same night
I'm having this dream . . .
Chocolate Cake and vanilla ice cream!
And though sure as hell I shall live to regret
it,
In that fabulous dream . . .
That's right . . .
I ate it!

The God Thing

They say God created man
In His own image.
Well, if He did,
Why did He make such a mess of it?
And not just a mess of us – the human race,
But of zillions more like us
Out there in space.
Unless of course they're better than us,
And we're His Pigs in a Poke,
His rejects,
God's little joke.

Far-fetched?
Well, maybe.
So tell me, then,
What's it all about?
Why are we born?
Why do we die?
Do *you* know?
No?
Nor do I.
One thing I *am* certain of –
God didn't create us.

How do I know?
Because God doesn't exist,
God forgive me for saying so.
Though I must admit
I'd prefer it
If He did.
Why?
Well, without God
There'd be no future,
Only the present and the past.
Meaning the day I breath my last
Will really be the end,
Which makes death very terminal, my friend.

But still, there's always one chance in a million,
Or in 13.8 billion,
That I could be wrong,
That I may not be the right singer,
That this may not be the right song.

So on my final day
I might well say
A quiet prayer,
Rather than risk losing face.
Just in case, you understand,
Just in case there's someone there.

Verse

Verse leads me
With no particular rhyme
Or reason,
Speeds me
In and out of time
And season,
Puts me in places
I never thought to be,
Shows me faces
I never thought to see.
Sometimes for better,
Sometimes for worse.
That's what verse
Does for me.

Who am I?

Who am I?
Does it matter
Who I am?
Do *you* know who you are?
Does anyone care?

Does anyone know
Where we came from?
Or where we go
From here?
Nowhere, I fear.

Control

Depressed by Corona?
Weary of violence?
Wishing you could call a pause
To fires, floods, hurricanes and wars?
Troubled by everything you see?
Longing to end the misery,
The boredom and the pain,
So you are never troubled
Ever again?

You need to understand
You hold the future of the world
There in your hand.
It takes courage,
It takes guts.
No ifs, my friend,
No buts.
Here's how
To make it end
Right now.

Close your eyes.
Count to three.
Aim your remote.
And . . .
Wait for it . . .

TURN OFF THE TV!

Who Cares?

They slaughtered eighty kids today.
I've eaten too much Christmas cake.
The last giraffe was shot in May.
And now I've got a stomach ache.

A week ago I lost my dad.
We'll celebrate the New Year soon.
My neighbour's son is on jihad.
My gardener's on his honeymoon.

A plane crashed in the Southern Med.
The upstairs loo has sprung a leak.
Over a hundred people dead.
The pound is getting really weak.

The doctor says I'm overweight.
Yemen's bombed to smithereens.
Cancer ops will have to wait.
Must be something in the genes.

Our Father Whichart

When you offer up a prayer
To Father Whichart in heaven,
Don't you ever wonder
How he came to be up there,
Sitting on God's throne?
This mysterious Father Whichart,
This complete unknown?

And now they say there's been a coup,
That Father **Who**art's won the war,
And Father Whichart is no more.
Well I think you simply changed your name,
Father Which, to Father Who.
And I refuse to play your game,
If it's all the same to you.

So I have checked my number plate,
Our Father Which, Our Father Who.
And let me give it to you straight.
You are not my heavenly father,
Either one of you.

Time's Up

There we are, lad,
Time's up, that's it.
You've had your ration,
Done your bit.
Had a great life, have you?
Excellent! Good to know.
Must be such a comfort
Now it's time to go.

You didn't expect it?
Can't believe it's true?
Tough on the wife?
And on the kids too?
Could it be cancelled?
Or maybe delayed?
Not for me to say, mate.
That's life, I'm afraid.

Terrible shock, is it?
Doesn't seem real?
Nobody warned you?
Know just how you feel.
Wish I could help you,
But that's how it goes.
Do I know where you're off to?
God alone knows.

Tomorrow

I'm going to sit down
Tomorrow,
And do something great.
Going to do it
Tomorrow,
Before it's too late.
Going to finish the book
I've been writing for years,
And move the whole planet
To laughter and tears.

I'm going to sit down
Tomorrow,
And do something great,
Going to do it
Tomorrow,
Before it's too late.
A treatment for cancer,
Even better – a cure.
And the billions that roll in
I shall give to the poor.

I'm going to sit down
Tomorrow,
And do something great,
Going to do it
Tomorrow,
Before it's too late.
I long to be famous,
So I've worked out a plan
To take over the world,
And become the top man.

I'm going to sit down
Tomorrow,
And do something great.
Going to do it
Tomorrow,
Before it's too late.
I'll definitely do it,
Don't you tell me I won't.
Going to do it – well –
Some day.
Just you see if I don't!

The Song of the Blackbird

My garden has many species
Of flowers and trees,
Birds and bees,
A Hindu, a Christian,
A Muslim, and a Jew.
Yes, and a blackbird too
Who sings to the others
The whole day long.
If only they would listen
To his song.

My Old Clock

There's my dear old clock
Standing in the hall.
Though I've never heard it chime,
Or seen it tell the time,
It's my favourite clock of all.
People ask me what it's got
That my other clocks do not,
And are amazed when I reply
'It's the one and only clock
On which I totally rely.'

My dear old clock is never fast,
Nor is it ever slow.
It stopped at ten to seven
Many a long year ago,
And whatever upset its innards,
I'm afraid I'll never know.
But I know when it's ten to seven
Every night and every day.
Yes, I know when it's ten to seven,
Whatever the other clocks say.

What Will I Do?

What will I do when I'm dead?
Whatever the pious ones say
I'm sure I'll be frantically bored
Contemplating my navel all day,
And saying my prayers to the Lord.

What will I do when I'm dead?
There won't be a TV in sight,
No doggies, no whisky, no friends,
Not a damn thing to do every night,
And endlessly barren weekends.

What will I do when I'm dead?
I'll miss summer and winter,
I'll miss autumn and spring,
I'll miss reading in bed.
I'll miss every damn thing.

So the answer, I fear,
Is depressingly clear.
When my lifetime is through
Above all, I'll miss you.

Which is why
I’ve decided
I am not going to die.

One Day They'll Come Knocking

One day they'll come knocking.
They'll beat down your door
And drag you away
To murder or enslave you,
Whatever you say,
Whatever you do.

When it comes to the end,
Will anyone be there?
Will anyone care?
Care enough to save you?
Will anyone dare?
Dare be your friend?

Just Once

Just once before I die
I'm going to fly.
Watch me leap
High, high, high
Into the woolly sky
Flocked with clouds of sheep.
And there I'll stay
Till the end of day.
And then I'll sleep.

Memories

They say
You can't take it with you.
Ok, then.
I'll just take my memories
When I go.

Ready?

I'm the first to admit,
That my life has been fun,
But I've packed all my kit,
So the day that it's done,
I'll be ready to blow.
I'll be ready, I'll be steady,
I'll be ready to go.

I'll cross all my fingers
And both of my thumbs,
While I wait for the bugle,
The roll of the drums.
I'll be ready to blow,
I'll be ready, I'll be steady,
I'll be ready to go.

The day that I pick up
My life load of stuff,
The day my heart tells me
Enough is enough,
On that day, I know,
I'll be ready, I'll be steady,
I'll be ready to go.

But then . . .
The first thing this morning
I pulled up the blind
To let in the sunlight.
And that changed my mind.
So it's got to be no!
It's got to be no!
I'll never be ready,
I'll never be steady!
I'll never be ready to go!

Remembrance

We remember those who died,
But not the reason why
They had to die.
We march to solemn music,
Lay our poppy wreaths,
Assume our doleful face.
But why did we send them
In the first place?

We packed them off to war:
Fathers,
Brothers,
Sons.
Do we know what for?
The sad truth is
No one remembers any more.

This and That

Maybe it's the way I played it,
Maybe it was meant to be,
But I never really made it
More than half way up the tree.
Jack of all trades I've been,
Master of none.
Though now I look back,
And when all's said and done,
Never really making it
Was a hell of a lot of fun.

With Apologies to William Blake

Tiger! Tiger! Burning bright
In the forests of the night,
What immortal hand or eye
Could frame thy fearful symmetry?

Tiger! Tiger! You must die!
We all know the reason why.
God made your organs, bones and skin
To use in Chinese Medicine!

Kill the lion!
Kill the lark!
Kill the walrus!
Kill the shark!
Kill the leopard!
Kill the dog!
Kill the monkey!
Kill the frog!
Kill everything in sight!
Kill by day, and kill by night!
The world will be a better place
When nothing's left
But the human race!

Tiger! Tiger! You must die!
We all know the reason why.
God made your organs, bones and skin
To use in Chinese Medicine!

Kill the rhino!
Kill the mole!
Kill the badger!
Kill the vole!
Kill the skylark!
Kill the bees!
Burn the land!
Cut down the trees!
Kill everything in sight!
Kill by day, and kill by night!
The world will be a better place
When nothing's left
But the human race!

Tiger! Tiger! You must die!
We all know the reason why.
God made your organs, bones and skin
To use in Chinese Medicine!

Kill the dolphin!
Kill the fowl!
Kill the otter!
Kill the owl!
Kill the elephant!
Kill the shrimp!

Kill the cheetah!
Kill the chimp!
Kill everything in sight!
Kill by day, and kill by night!
The world will be a better place
When nothing's left
But the human race!

Tiger! Tiger! You must die!
We all know the reason why.
God made your organs, bones and skin
To use in Chinese Medicine!

Tiger! Tiger! Burning bright
In the forests of the night,
What immortal hand or eye
Could frame thy fearful symmetry?

It's Late

It's late, it's late.
It's getting very late.
It's been a blast,
But time goes fast.
It doesn't wait.
I'll soon be past
My sell by date.

The Inescapable Truth

The truth that is completely true,
The one that catches up with you,
Is the truth that however hard you try
One of these days you are going to die.

Life

I've seen it, seen it all,
Seen what is,
Seen what might have been,
Seen that other life, what's more,
In a mirror on the wall,
Through an open door.
Oh yes, I've seen it,
Seen it all.

I've seen it, seen it all,
Seen what is,
Seen what might have been.
Seen in my day
The very worst,
And yes, the very best of it.
Wish I could stay
To see the rest of it.

The Good Old Days

We all look back to the old days,
To the golden days we knew,
When the sun was always shining,
And the sky was always blue.

But if those good as gold days
Would come again somehow,
Would they really be as golden
As the days we're living now?

Where Will They Run To?

Where will they run to?
Where will they hide?
When all the seas are poisoned,
And all the trees have died?

Will they look for a new world,
Knowing it won't be long
Before the sun sets for ever
On the blackbird's song?

Will they find another planet
Somewhere out in space,
Destined to be ravaged
By the human race?

Yesterday

Do I remember yesterday?
Why yes, of course I do!
The places that I went to,
The people that I knew.
The memories may have faded,
The recall may be slow.
But then yesterday –
Well it seems like only yesterday –
Yesterday was a long, long time ago.

Tweet Tweet

You wouldn't believe it,
You couldn't conceive it,
But someone just tweeted
The meaning of life!
So I'm out on the street,
And I scream and I yell,
'Up there is heaven!
Down there is hell!
I know why we live!
I know why we die!
I've just had the call!
I know the whole story.
The tweet said it all!'

Some whistled and cheered.
Some sniggered and jeered.
Some stood there and stared,
And some acted scared.
Then one man cried, 'Cheat!
You're infected with Tweet!
I'll have you reported
If you don't get it sorted'.

So I go to my doctor,
Who gives it me straight.
Says he's terribly sorry,
But I've left it too late.
How he wished people knew
The harm tweeting can do.
For a tweet, once it's caught,
Paralyses all thought.
I can never be treated.
I'm incurably tweeted.

What's the Real Story?

Believers tell us we should just
Take our little lives on trust.
No point, they say, in asking why –
Why we're born,
Or why we die.

All we need to understand
Is that the universe is planned,
That life and death are never chance,
And nothing is mere happenstance.

Well, those believers may be right,
And I might live to see the light.
But being a pawn in someone's game
I'd like to know who's playing it,
And how it's going to end.
If it's all the same
To You,
My Reticent Friend.

Old Age

It's really hard to keep your feet
When everywhere you go
The whole damned world around you
Is swaying to and fro.

Our country, so the government claims,
Is stable and secure.
So how come it won't stop shaking
If they're so damn sure?

It's the usual lies and double talk
That frankly make me sick.
Next time I go out walking
I'll take a bloody stick.

Which Is It?

After all these years
I still don't know if I'm
A Doubting Believer,
Or a Believing Doubter.
Will I ever find out?
I doubt it.

I am I

I am I.
I am the reason why.
I am, for better or for worse,
The centre of the universe.
I am the present and the past.
I am the first one, and the last.
I am every night and day.
I am the only chosen way.
I am my enemy and my friend.
I am the beginning,
And the end.
I am the reason why.
I am I.

Goodbye

Time to let him go,
That's what they said.
And I said yes,
Wanting to say no.
So they slid the needle in,
And my beloved dog was dead.

Kill Death

I am strongly opposed to this death business,
A problem we all have to face.
Let us deal with it now, or risk saying
Goodbye to the whole human race.

I suggest you complain to your Council,
And write to your local MP
To insist on your right to be granted
A statutory opt-out for free.

Let's demand that the idiots we vote for
Explain to us instantly why,
With our twenty-first century know-how
Anybody on earth needs to die.

It's time we did something about it.
I urge you to answer the call.
We'd all be much better off without it.
Let's kill off death once and for all.

True Love

We met in a Carphone Warehouse.
I went there to update my phone,
When I saw standing there in a corner,
Standing completely alone,
This ravishing, radiant beauty,
The most glamorous I ever have known.

And it was love, love, love at first sight,
It was love, love, love that was right.
It was love every day, It was love every night.
Now we're always together, I love her so much.
She glows like the sun at my fingertips' touch.

Now, of course, there are millions of cynics who
say
That love, like a fever, burns out in a day.
Well they'll change their opinion the moment
they see
We're still madly in love when we're old and
we're gray –
My very own,
Mobile Phone,
And me.

If

If I had played the piano,
Or strummed on a guitar,
I would have topped the music charts,
And been a star.

If I had been a climber
I would have climbed so high
I'd have stood on the peak of Everest,
And touched the sky.

If I had been a writer
It would come as no surprise
When the Academy awarded me
The Nobel Prize.

If I had been a sculptor,
I'd be sculptor to the Crown,
With a life size statue of myself
In every town.

Mind you – if I were famous,
Would anyone give a damn?
Maybe I should just be satisfied
With what I am.

Jin No Wad Amin?

He was, they say, the greatest king
The world has ever seen.
Worshipped as a demi-god –
Jin No Wad Amin!

The most famous woman in the world,
The emperor's lovely queen,
As wise as she was beautiful –
No Wad Amin!

A more devoted wife than her
They said has never been.
And she was the only one for him –
Jin No Wad Amin!

Sadly it was just a fantasy.
They hated each other's guts.
He was a chronic psychopath.
And she was completely nuts.

. . . Jin No Wad Amin?

It Really Is a Problem

Have a nice day. No problem.
Can I speak to . . . ?
No problem.
The world is choked with plastic.
No problem.
I loathe your tattoos.
No problem.
I loathe you too.
No problem.
Good morning.
No problem.
Good afternoon.
No problem.
Good night.
No problem.

I have cancer.
No problem.
You have cancer.
No problem.
Get stuffed.
No problem.
I'm going to cash in your pension.

No problem.
I'm going to smash in your face.
No problem.
I'm going to murder you online.
No problem.

Well, I have a problem.
No problem.
Why is everything no problem?
No problem.

A Grain of Truth?

In the next ten thousand years
On some deserted beach
There'll be a billion grains of sand
Washed in by the sea.
And one of them
Will be me.

The Conjuror

Like a conjuror,
From time to time
I dip into my hat,
And flip – Hey Presto! –
A memory of this and that –
A special song,
A favourite book,
A photograph.
Could that be us?
How young we look.
For just a moment
Then is now,
And now is then.

Wish we could have it all again.

Now and Then

Dozing in the garden
Under a tree,
Much loved doggy
On my knee.

This is today.
Who cares
Where or what I'll be,
The why, the wherefore and the how
A million years from now?
Not my doggy –
Or me.

What's the Point?

No point asking questions
When there's no way of knowing
How the whole story started,
Or where it's all going.

Can it possibly matter
What you choose to believe
When one day you arrive,
And the next one you leave?

Autumn

With the dark nights closing in –
The long, dark winter nights –
I dream of
Bluebells and buttercups,
Roses and sunflowers.
Can't wait to feel the sun
Dismiss the winter chill.

I expect I will.

The Song

There were times when I got it right,
And times when I got it wrong.
I may have sung it out of tune,
But at least I sang the song.

Mister Blackbird

Tell me, Mister Blackbird,
Tell me, tell me true,
Sitting on the garden fence,
Who are you singing to?

Is it to the rising moon?
Or the dying day?
Is it to your blackbird friends?
Or the Milky Way?

Tell me, Mister Blackbird,
Tell me, could it be,
Sitting on the garden fence,
That you are singing to me?

Old Age

Frankly it's driving me round the bend,
Not to mention up the wall.
Me and old age – we don't get on,
We don't get on at all.
I'll never get used to the bloody thing,
Or change the way I feel.
Mind you,
When I consider the alternative,
It doesn't appeal.

Dog Help Me

Are there any dogs in heaven?
That's what I'd like to know.
If I can have a dog up there
It's where I'm going to go.

If I am not allowed a dog
I won't be coming to stay.
I'll think of somewhere else to go.
I'll find some other way.

But if You'd let me have a dog
I'd be grateful to the end.
We'd worship and adore You –
Me and my doggie friend.

A Cautionary, like, Tale

So I meets this, like, gorgeous chick,
And I, like, I says to her . . .
Well, you know how it is, like.
And she was, like.
You wouldn't, like, believe it.
We were, like, both of us
Like, over the moon.
Ginowhaddamin? –
Both of us, like,
We, like, knew exactly,
Knew it was, like, always,
Meant, like, to be.
So, wajado?
She was, like,
And I was, like.
So I, like, married her,
Married her, like, the same day.
And, like, the next day.
She, like, left me.
Funny. Wonnit?
Like.

Departed Friends

At the bottom of the garden
Beneath the willow tree
Lie the remains of all the dogs
Who shared my life with me.

And in my mind they share it still.
And still I share their play,
The licks, the leaps, the joy with which
They welcome every day.

In my memory those precious dogs
I shall forever keep.
Until the day we meet again
Sleep, little dogs, sleep.

OCD

Take my advice, my friend, do not delay!
Do it now! Do it today!
It's vital not to hesitate!
Tomorrow will be far too late.
So get your life in order.
Get it straight!

Your walk,
Your talk,
Your knife
And fork,
Your spoon,
Your plate,
Your garden gate,
Your table,
Your chair,
Your tie,
Your hair.
Your shoes,
Your socks,
Your antique clocks.
Ignore the temptations of the devil,
And keep the pictures on your wall precisely level!

So listen to me, friend, and listen well.
Make sure your life is parallel.
Or, when you die,
You will go straight for once –
Straight to hell!

Lockdown

It's gone.
Disappeared.
Just like that.
Who would have thought it?
Vanished into thin air.
Must be somewhere.
Here or there.
But where?
Where, oh where?
Oh, where can it be?
I had it yesterday.
And the day before.
Didn't I?
I'm *sure* I did.
I *know* I did.

What's more, I know
I had it weeks ago. Weeks ago!
What am I saying? I had it last year.
I'm *sure* I did.
I *know* I did!
And the year before that.
Or was it two?
Things turn up of course.
They always do.
Got to be somewhere.
Here or there.
But where?
Where oh where can it be?
Where is my life?
Someone has stolen it from me!

Love

It's all about love, Isn't it?
About what we feel.
It's the only thing that's real.
All the rest
Is shit.
Isn't it?

Democracy

We vote for left,
We vote for right.
One lot give us day,
The other night.
Some are do-ers.
Some are die-ers.
One thing they have in common -
They're all of them effing liars.

Apologies to W. S. Gilbert

On a tree by a river a little tom-tit
Sang Whitty, titWhitty, titWhitty!
And I said to him, 'Dicky-bird, why do sit
Singing Whitty, titWhitty, titWhitty?'

'The look on your face is as grim as the grave.
Can't you cheer us all up with a smile and a wave?'
'Don't you know,' Whitty moaned, 'being Boris's slave
Is shitty! So shitty! So shitty!'

'May we ask you, titWhitty, why you never disclose
The point of the merciless rules you impose?
Your Lock-up's a Cock-up as everyone knows,
Show pity! titWhitty. Show pity!'

'I am trapped and tormented and racked by despair.
I shall die of frustration and boredom, I swear.'

'If you don't die of Covid, why the hell should I care?'
Said Whitty, titWhitty, titWhitty!

Saving Lives?

Saving lives! Saving lives!
That's why we're told we cannot meet –
Parents, children, husbands, wives –
In our houses, in the street.

Saving lives! Saving lives!
Locked inside a prison cell,
Parents, children, husbands, wives –
Life's become a living hell.

Saving lives! Saving lives!
And when we have our lives again –
Parents, children, husbands, wives –
What kind of lives will we have then?

Land of Hope and Glory

Land of Hope and Glory,
Mother of the free –
That used to be the story –
How it was meant to be.

In our Land of Hope and Glory
The infamous three –
Boris, Matt and Twitty –
Stole our liberty.

Wider still and wider
Shall our bounds be set.
But maximum two meters –
And don't you dare forget.

Or larger still and larger
Will your penalties be,
And you will be in lockup
For all eternity.

Tiers!

Tiers! Tiers! Tiers!
They can't stop shedding Tiers!
They come in a perpetual flood,
And every Tier's as clear as mud.
So Cheers! Boris! Cheers!

If I'm on One, and you're on Two,
They say I'm better off than you.
But I know this guy who's on Tier three,
And he gets all his booze for free.
So Cheers! Boris! Cheers!

I had a crazy dream last night,
Fearsome, weird and wild.
Boris got his figures right.
And Twitty smiled.
So Tiers! Boris! Tiers!

Boris! Boris!

(to the tune of Daisy, Daisy)

Bo-ris! Bo-ris!
Never knows what to do!
Why keep changing,
Driving us all cuckoo?
Today it's the circuit-breaker,
Or a trip to the undertaker.
The one thing, I fear,
You have made crystal clear –
You do not have a bloody clue!

Ah . . . Tissue!

Will some kind person tell me please
What compels my dog to sneeze?
It could be, I suppose,
A problem with his nose.
But I'm obliged to wipe it,
When I'd really like to swipe it.

Whilst I'm willing to agree
That this problem may not be
The most important issue
Of our times,
At least it rhymes.

The Willow Tree

The willow in my garden
Celebrating spring, waves
Its bright green curtain
Over my doggies' graves.

Whispers to them gently
Springtime's joyful news –
Wake up! The winter's over!
Wake up! No time to lose!

Listen to me, doggies!
It's time to run and play!
What's the point of sleeping
Day after day?

I wake up every springtime
Though I sleep the winter through.
Tell me little doggies,
Why can't you?

How To Be Famous!

I'd like to be a movie star.
I'd like to drive a fancy car.
I'd like to be a billionaire.
I'd like to dance like Fred Astaire.
I'd like to wear a royal crown.
I'd like the biggest house in town.
I'd like to conquer Everest.
I'd like to have a hairy chest.

But if I can't,
I can always be
A talentless

CELEBRITY!!!!

The Circle of Life

Philosophers say that life's a circle
With no beginning, and no end.
And whatever we passed by yesterday
Is waiting for us round the bend.
So the day my life and I are parted
I won't have to worry about a thing,
'Cos I'll soon be right back where I started,
Which, to say the least, is comforting.

Mr Neverwas

Everything he said he'd done
He didn't.
Every game he said he'd won
He hadn't.
Everything he said he'd seen
He never did.
Everywhere he said he'd been
He wasn't.
Every time he said he could
He couldn't.
Every time he said he would
He wouldn't.
Everything he said he was
He wasn't.
You knew exactly
Where you weren't
With Mr Neverwas.

Time to Woke up?

It's time to rebel,
Time to send all prejudice to hell,
Time to heal, time to mend,
Time for cruelty to end,
Time to be strong, time to be bold,
Time to break the stranglehold
Of men on women,
White on black, Straight on gay,
It's time to get our freedom back,
Time to celebrate a brand new day.
Hip Pip! Hip Pip! Hip Hip! Hooray!

Now let the golden age begin.
Out with the Out!
In with the In!

Reject the Unwoke	Embrace the Woke
Masterly	Missterly
Master key	Misses key
Master craftsman	Misses craftsman
Man-of-war	Woman-of-war
Manchester	Womanchester
Manic	Womanic
Manipulate	Womanipulate
Romantic	Rowomantic
Black hole	White hole
Blackberry	White berry
Black and Tan	White and Tan
Black cab	White cab
Black Sea	White Sea
Blacken a name	Whiten a name
Blacksmith	Whitesmith
Baa baa black sheep	Baa baa white sheep
Blackpool	Whitepool

Gay Gordon's	Heterosexual Gordon's
Straight laced	Gay Laced
Straight away	Gay away
I'll have it straight up	I'll have it gay up
The straight and narrow	The gay and narrow

And we're all quite sane!

Or are we?

Books by Alan Fenton

Shadow of the Titan

The Call of Destiny

The Hour of Camelot

Kill or be Killed